THE FLORIDA KEYS

ISLANDS IN THE SEA

William Russell

The Rourke Book Co., Inc.
Vero Beach, Florida 32964

Edited by Sandra A. Robinson

PHOTO CREDITS
© Lynn M. Stone: pages 10, 12, 13, 17; courtesy of Monroe County
Tourist Development Council: cover, title page, pages 7, 8, 18;
courtesy of Florida Division of Tourism: page 4; © Mary A. Cote,
page 15

Library of Congress Cataloging-in-Publication Data

Russell, William, 1942-
   The Florida Keys / by William Russell.
      p. cm. — (Islands in the sea)
   Includes index.
   ISBN 1-55916-032-2
   1. Florida Keys (Fla.)—Juvenile literature. [1. Florida Keys (Fla.)]
I. Title. II. Series.
F317.M7R87 1994
975.9'41—dc20   93-48334
                                    CIP

Printed in the USA   AC

TABLE OF CONTENTS

THE FLORIDA KEYS

The Florida Keys are a chain of small, low-lying islands off the southern tip of Florida. Like a long string of green beads, they reach about 150 miles southwest into the Atlantic Ocean.

Early Spanish explorers called these islands *cayos* — "little islands." English-speaking people changed the word to "keys."

The Florida Keys have colorful undersea gardens of bright fish and **coral.** The Keys also have unusual wildlife and excellent sport fishing.

A fisherman reels in his prize off Islamorada in the Florida Keys

THE KEYS OF CORAL

Many of the Florida Keys are made of coral rock. Corals are small **marine,** or sea, creatures that live in warm oceans.

Corals produce a liquid that hardens into "rock." Many corals live together and build huge structures of rock. These rough, rocky structures are called **coral reefs.**

Some of the reefs lie close to the ocean surface. In the past, hurricanes often blew sailing ships onto the reefs. The reefs of the Keys are a graveyard for old Spanish ships.

Divers swim with colorful fish at John Pennekamp Coral Reef State Park off Key Largo

THE KEYS LONG AGO

The Keys have a past filled with lively stories. Calusa Indians once lived in the Keys. Pirates used the islands for hideouts.

In the 1800s, people known as wreckers got rich in the Keys. Wreckers saved goods from ships that storms crashed on the rocky reefs. "God has been good to us," the wreckers used to say. "He has sent us a wreck."

' Cigar makers, sea turtle hunters and sponge fishermen also had good fortune — and bad — in the old Keys.

Treasure hunter Mel Fisher and his team have found millions of dollars worth of gold that sank long ago with Spanish ships on the Keys' reefs

PEOPLE IN THE KEYS

People who live in the Lower Keys — those farthest from the Florida mainland — call themselves "conchs." Some of the early "conchs" were pirates — Black Caesar, Blackbeard and Sir Henry Morgan were some of the most famous. Ernest Hemingway, one of America's greatest writers, was a "conch" in the 1940s and 1950s.

Conchs are actually marine snails. Cooking recipes in the Lower Keys have conch snails in everything from chowders to salads.

A floating house for "conchs" is not unusual in Key West, where the lifestyle is relaxed

In the Crocodile National Wildlife Refuge on Key Largo,
an American crocodile helps warm itself by opening its jaws

A great white heron watches over Bahia Honda State Park in the Lower Keys

SEAS AROUND THE KEYS

The blue-green seas around the Florida Keys attract sport fishermen, boaters, **snorkelers,** divers and treasure hunters. Mel Fisher and his crew have found millions of dollars worth of sunken Spanish treasure.

Almost everyone who visits or lives in the Keys enjoys water sports. Snorkelers and divers love John Pennekamp Coral Reef State Park, one of several living reefs in the Keys. Pennekamp was the first undersea park in America. Over 650 kinds of fish and 40 kinds of coral live on the reef.

Related to jellyfish, corals use tentacles to catch tiny prey

VISITING THE KEYS

Visitors find the beauty of the Keys in the sea, instead of the land. The shores of the Keys are mostly rocky or muddy.

Much of the jungle that used to cover the Keys has been cleared. Many of the Keys have town centers.

A few of the Keys do remain forested and without roads or residents. One is Lignumvitae Key, which the state of Florida protects from change.

16

This nature trail in Key Deer National Wildlife Refuge leads through a forest of pine and palmetto on Big Pine Key

THE OVERSEAS HIGHWAY

The road to the Keys is the remarkable Overseas Highway. The highway's 42 bridges — one of them seven miles long — link 32 Keys.

The highway stretches from the Florida mainland to Key West, 128 miles southwest. The road follows the route of Henry Flagler's old railway to Key West. In 1935, a hurricane destroyed the railroad's path just 23 years after it was built.

The Seven-Mile Bridge is part of the Overseas Highway, the southern tip of U.S. Route 1, which begins in Maine

KEY WEST

Key West isn't quite the end of the Keys, but it is the end of the road.

In 1838, Key West was the largest and busiest town in Florida. Today, Key West is a small town busy with **tourists,** or visitors. The town's old buildings, sunset views and relaxed lifestyle make it popular. Many tourists drive to Key West just because it is the last stop along the Overseas Highway. Cuba is only 90 miles away.

WILDLIFE OF THE KEYS

Some of America's rarest wild animals live in the woodlands and swamps of the Florida Keys. One unusual creature is the shy American crocodile. A national wildlife **refuge** on Key Largo helps protect the crocs.

Another refuge in the Lower Keys helps protect the tiny Key deer. A full-grown Key deer is the size of a collie dog!

Some other rare and unusual animals of the Keys are tree-climbing snails and crabs, roseate spoonbills, reddish egrets and great white herons.

Glossary

coral (KOR ul) — any one of several kinds of soft, simple marine animals, many of which build rocky reefs

coral reef (KOR ul REEF) — a large, rocky, undersea structure built by certain coral animals

marine (muh REEN) — of or relating to the sea, salt water

refuge (REH fewj) — a safe place; an area overseen by the U.S. Fish and Wildlife Service for the protection of certain wild animals

snorkeler (SNOR kel er) — a person who swims with the help of a snorkel, a special breathing tube

tourist (TOUR ihst) — a person who visits a place to see and learn about it

INDEX